How to Tawlk and Rite Good

Anna—
Hope this book larns
you rite good!

Sam Venable
5/6/17

Also by Sam Venable

An Island Unto Itself

A Handful of Thumbs and Two Left Feet

Two or Three Degrees Off Plumb

One Size Fits All and Other Holiday Myths

From Ridgetops to Riverbottoms: A Celebration of the Outdoor Life in Tennessee

I'd Rather Be Ugly than Stuppid

Mountain Hands: A Portrait of Southern Appalachia

Rock-Elephant: A Story of Friendship and Fishing

You Gotta Laugh to Keep from Cryin': A Baby Boomer Contemplates Life beyond Fifty

Someday I May Find Honest Work: A Newspaper Humorist's Life

WARNING! This Product Contains Nuttiness: A Fun Look at the Bizarre World in Which We Live

"Talk Is Cheap" comedy tour holiday edition DVD (recorded at the Museum of Appalachia in Norris, Tenn.)

How to Tawlk and Rite Good

A guide to the language of Southern Appalachia

Sam Venable

This effort is dedicated to the many teachers, formally educated and otherwise, who done learnt me to tawlk and rite good.

INTRODUCTION

As proof of the sad level of mediocrity to which the University of Tennessee and the National Park Service have sunk, my wife and I are hired each summer to teach locals and tourists at the Smoky Mountain Field School in Sugarlands Visitors Center. Our "specialty" (I use the term loosely) is mountain heritage and dialect.

In other words, "How to tawlk and rite good."

I always stress at the start of every class that my "expertise" is solely that of a layman blessed with the ability to detect and interpret dialect. Nothing more.

I'm trained as a journalist with a background in forestry and wildlife management; Mary Ann specialized in software education throughout her long career in the private sector and at UT. But we both are natives with good ears (or "years," as the case may be) who grew up in the shadow of these mountains.

If students are looking for scholarly instruction into the roots of Southern Appalachian speech patterns, they need to study research by the sure-nuff experts: the late Cratis Williams of Appalachian State University in Boone, N.C., and Dr. Michael Montgomery of the University of South Carolina, to name just a couple. To educationally paraphrase our differences: I know how to use crawdads to "ketch bass;" they know how to scientifically dissect crayfish.

The language I like to call "hillbillyeze" is not a Deep South drawl. You'd never confuse it with, say, the lilting verse of

Charleston, S.C., the Creole-Cajun French of coastal Louisiana or the syrup of sweet-home Alabama. I'm convinced that the speech patterns of my home region are a mixture of Elizabethan English, Scots-Irish, German, Swiss, French and God-only-knows-what-else, blended and softened by 100-proof mountain twang. It's the language I grew up hearing, and I miss it.

No, I don't propose a return to caricatured images of barefoot mountaineers swigging 'shine from a jug. But we *are* losing this delightful form of oral and written communication. It pains me that the true mother tongue of America is now alleged to be that of a Midwestern newscaster. No drawl. No dropping the "'g" at the end of active verbs. No mispronounced words like "adder" for "after." No hacksawed terms like "'backer" for "tobacco." Aaak! Spare me! Perhaps half a century from now, when "Southern Appalachese" no longer rings through these ridges and valleys, a handful of renegades will still "tawlk and rite good." We can only hope.

I suppose there are enough Southern Appalachian "tawlkin'" and "ritin'" words to fill a 500-page dictionary. What follows are just a few of my favorites. Some are humorous adaptations I often use in standup routines on the "Talk Is Cheap" comedy tour that I perform with three other regional entertainers: Bill Landry, Elizabeth Rose and Jimmy Claborn. Others are listed exactly as they are spoken in the hill country.

Here, then, is the language of my people. I hope you enjoy it.

Sam Venable
August 11, 2013

A

a'—Emphasis added to any active verb. *I'm a'fixin' to call in sick, then go a'fishin'.*

Abidy—Person. *Hit's a'fixing to come a cloud; abidy shore could git soaked.*

Acrost—Correct pronunciation of "across." *During the big flood last sprang, Ike got acrost his bridge jest afore hit collapsed.*

Adder—At a later time. *I told Maw I'd fix the roof adder turkey season.*

Afeered—Correct pronunciation of "afraid," specifically used in the context of "suspect." *From the looks of how she fills out 'at weddin' dress, I'm afeered the bride may be jest the least bit pregnant.*

Afore—Correct pronunciation of "before." *Afore we walk any deeper into these here woods, you might art to look at the map.*

Again—Opposed to. *The mayor's again ever proposal that comes afore City Council.*

Aholt—Cling to tightly. *Grab aholt of this rope!*

Aigs—Poultry products often consumed at breakfast. *Sometimes country people call aigs "cackleburries."*

Aim—Intend to. *I aim to go to town someday next week.*

Ain't—1. Your mother or father's sister. *Ain't June done baked us a peach pie.* 2. A tiny insect. *Don't step on 'em poor li'l ol' ain'ts!*

Air—Time period of 60 minutes. *Onct ol' Venable gits to talkin' he kin go on fer an air and hardly draw a breath.*

Airish—Chilly. *Hit shore has turned airish fer July!*

Airy—Correct pronunciation of "any." *Is thar airy cornmeal in 'at cubbard?*

All—Thick liquid used in engines. *My ol' Ford was so low on all, hit tuck four quarts!*

All git out—A high level, usually involving volatile emotion. *Jabbo was sadder'n all git out when his boy got kilt in the war.*

Allus—Correct pronunciation of "always." *Bad stuff allus happens on Friday the 13th.*

Anothern—One more. *I'd already done et two, but when Poovie past 'em biscuits around, I jest grabbed me anothern.*

Anywhores—Correct pronunciation of "anywhere." *You kin look anywhores in this county and still not find better vittles than Ruth Ann's.*

Apern—Dress covering worn while cooking. *When she made dumplin's, Ain't Laura allus got flare on her apern.*

Aplenty—Sufficient. *I've had aplenty of aigs fer breakfast.*

Arn—1. Metal. *Phil's head is hard as arn.* 2. Garment-pressing. *I ast Maw to please arn my best shirt.*

Arnry—Contrary. *I swear Ain't Lizzie is as arnry as airy wommin I ever seed!*

Aromatic—A gun capable of rapid fire. *Ralph's aromatic Remington shoots fast as he kin pull the trigger.*

Arrol—Projectile used in archery. *Looks like ol' Cupid done shot an arrol rat through Sue Ellen's heart!*

Arsh—A white potato. *I like arsh taters better'n sweet taters.*

Art—Correct pronunciation of "ought." *If you want to know how to tawlk and rite good, you art to buy Sam Venable's book!*

Ar-tickle—Correct pronunciation of "article." *When John got hisself arrested fer thievin', they run an ar-tickle about him in the newspaper.*

Assahole—Common term to unite various parts of a larger unit. *Politicians, assahole, will say dam near anything to git reelected.*

Assbackards—In reverse. *Otto was so dumb, he couldn't even spell his name assbackards.*

Assle—Foolish waste of time. *Walter assled around so long he missed his ride to the store.*

Asspern—Common over-the-counter medication for pain. *Doc Jenkins told me to take two asspern and call him in the mornin'.*

Ast—Correct pronunciation of "ask." *He ast fer her hand in marriage.*

Asteroids—A painful rectal ailment. *Paw had asteroids so bad, he went out and bought ever tube of Preparation H they was in town.*

'at—Correct pronunciation of "that." *Adder he drunk all 'at bellywarsh, Herb's boy was about to bust, so he peed on 'at oak tree over yonder.*

Atall—Correct pronunciation of "at all." *He don't have nary teeth in his mouth atall.*

B

'Backer—Tobacco. *Annie Lou grows a right smart crop of 'backer ever year.*

Backslide—To lose personal convictions, especially of a religious nature. *Onct Bill got 'at big city job, he started backslidin' and don't hardly ever come to church no more.*

Bad-sick—Exceedingly ill. *Liz tuck bad-sick, and thar fer the longest time I thought she was a goner.*

Bag—To plead. *No matter how much Amy would bag him to stop, Russell kept on a'drankin' likker.*

Bale—Correct pronunciation of "bell." *Whew! I shore wish 'at dinner bale would rang!*

Banch—Furniture used for sitting. *We done run outta cheers; you kin jest sit over yonder on 'at banch.*

Banjer—A popular musical instrument. *My friend Larry learnt Doc Nevils to play a banjer rail good.*

Bank walker—A well-endowed young man casually showing off his "manhood" at the swimming hole. *Perry was a shore-nuff bank walker. The rest of us allus had t'jump in rail quick and hope the water was muddy!*

Bard—Past tense of "borrow." *I bard $10 from Frank 'til payday.*

Barium—What you do to people after they die. *Billy and Janet, bless their hearts, died in 'at car crash together, so we're gonna barium together.*

Barl—1. A large container for liquids. *They's a rain barl a'settin' on the front porch.* 2. Part of a gun through which projectiles are launched. *Allen's ol' hawg rifle had a 20-inch barl.*

Barley—Correct pronunciation of "barely." *Luther barley made hit home afore the storm.*

Bat trees—Power packs for portable devices. *I need to buy some AA bat trees fer my raddeo.*

Bate—1. Any material, preferably live, used to catch fish. *I allus bate with minners when I fish fer crappies.* 2. A large portion. *You kin allus count on Hoss to eat a bate of fried crappies.*

Beatin'est—High praise for a task well done. *Muggins caught the beatin'est limit of trout ever I seed. Why, I bet the least'un was 15 inches!*

Beautious—Gorgeous. *If they ain't nary fog, sunrise at Myrtle Point is a beautious thang.*

Bellywarsh—Any kind of soft drink. *I like Big Arnj bellywarsh the best.*

Benz—Another term for "Since you are—." *Benz how yore a'goan to Gatlinburg in the first place, do you care to buy me a few boxes of taffy?*

Berd—Long facial hair growth. *J.R. ain't shaved his berd since 1968.*

Bidness—Type of work, especially a professional occupation. *Bill Bob cut some kinda bidness deal with the guvermit.*

Big Arnj—1. Popular soft drink. *I allus drink a Big Arnj at the football game.* 2. Nickname for University of Tennessee athletic teams. *I allus root fer the Big Arnj, even when they git their asses kicked.*

Biggurn—Anything large, preferably of a game or fish nature. *Roy's walleye shore was a biggurn!*

Bile—Correct pronunciation of "boil." *Water will bile at 212 degrees.*

Bire—Large black furry animals often seen in the Smokies, usually mispronounced "bar" by ignorant Yankees and Hollywood scriptwriters hoping to impress the natives. *Bire season opens next weekend.*

Bleef—A devoutly held conviction. *Marge had a firm bleef in the pare of prayer.*

Bless his/her/their heart(s)—Expression of kindliness offered about people you're about to disparage. *Jonah, bless his heart, ain't done an honest day's work in his life.*

Blowed—Past tense of "blew." *Sarah blowed the candle out and went to bed.*

Bobacue—Pork (and only pork!) slowly smoked for hours over hickory coals; not to be confused with "barbecue," a term Yankees apply to any meat—hotdogs to hamburgers—quickly charred on a $4 K-mart grill. *I believe Eugene's bobacue could win one of 'em contests in Memphis.*

Bobwar—Metallic fencing material that comes in large coils. *Carl strung five strands of bobwar 'round his feed lot.*

Bofus—Two people acting as one. *Bofus are fixin' to go a'fishin' on Saturday.*

Bones—Common nickname for a tall, skinny man. *Anytime Bones turned sideways in the wind, he whistled.*

Borned days—The entirety of one's life. *In all my borned days, I ain't never seed a wommin 'at purty!*

Borry—Lend. *Will you borry me a quarter?*

Boxcar letters—Large print. *Bert couldn't read his name in boxcar letters.*

Brane—Gray matter inside the skull. *If Roger had half a brane, he'd know Edna warnt his type.*

Bresh—Correct pronunciation of "brush." *Doris paid $5 fer her new hairbresh.*

Brethern/sistern—Brothers and sisters. *Brethern and sistern, let us pray.*

Brickle—Correct pronunciation of "brittle." *Be xtree careful a'climbin' 'at tree. Hits limbs shore look brickle to me.*

Brung—Past tense of "bring." *She brung me a loaf of light bread.*

Bubs—1. What you plant for iris and tulips. *Our flares are purty thanks to the good bubs we planted last fall.* 2. Sources of artificial light. *'Em new "squiggly" bubs shore take thar time a'lightin' up!*

Bum—An explosive device used in warfare. *When we dropped the A-bum on Japan, hit brought World War II to a quick end.*

Bumfuzzled—Confused. *I got all bumfuzzled when the teacher ast me to rite on the chalkboard.*

Burries—Any type of small fruit. *This has shore been a good summer fer blackburries.*

By grab!—A more polite way of saying, "By God!" *By grab! Cuzzin Earl kin shore sang a tune!*

C

Calf slobbers–Meringue, also any kind of thick pastry icing. *I bet the calf slobbers on 'at lemon pie was two inches tall!*

Call–Reason. *The principal had no call to make Johnny stay adder school.*

Cam–Correct pronunciation of "calm." *Adder 'at big storm we had last night, the wind shore is cam this mornin'.*

Camer-box–Photographic equipment. *Phyllis bought one of 'em new dijikal camer-boxes.*

Can to can't–Pre-dawn until after dark; i.e., from when the sun could be seen until it couldn't. *Bossman John eggpected us to dig holes from can to can't.*

Care-akter–Correct pronunciation of "character;" i.e., a delightful, humorous person. *Ol' Barney is such a care-akter! Everbidy in town loves him.*

Carn–Mountain pronunciation of "carrion." *Whew! 'At dead cat stanks like carn! Go sprankle some lime on hit!*

Cheer–Furniture used for sitting. *Draw up a cheer and have some dinner with us.*

Chillen–Correct pronunciation of "children." *The Houstons had so many chillen, I finally quit a'countin'.*

Chimley–Stone or metal device for exhausting smoke. *How you reckon Sainty Clause gits down the chimley?*

Choke with shoe dust–Run as fast as possible. *If 'at tush hawg Hodges boy comes a'lookin' fer me, Ima-goan choke him with shoe dust.*

Churched–Having church membership revoked. *Will cussed and drank and carried on with wild women so much, they finally churched him.*

Ciffer—Add, subtract, multiply, divide. *I can't hardly ciffer no more 'less I got one of 'em new dijikal addin' machines like they sell fer $2 down at the Sebmlebm.*

Clean—Completely. *I clean fergot to buy a new fishin' license!*

Clem—Past tense of "climb." *We clem 'at ridge 'til our tongues lolled out.*

Clinics—Paper hand tissues. *They had a box of clinics on ever pew at Ain't Mollie's funeral.*

Close line—A rope used for drying clothing. *Paula strung a close line in her backyard.*

Co-Cola—A famous brand of soft drink. *You kin buy a Co-Cola anywhores in the world!*

Cogigate—To think deeply. *I'll have to cogigate on 'at fer a while.*

Cole all—Kerosene. *Don't put Coleman fuel in 'at lantern! Hit uses cole all! You'll blow us all to smithereens!*

Colyum—Regularly appearing feature in a newspaper or magazine. *Sam Venable's colymn in the News Sentinel runs Tuesdays, Thursdays, Fridays and Sundays.*

Cordin—Correct pronunciation of "according." *Cordin to my bank balance, I've been a'spendin' money like Congress.*

Course—To follow, usually by sound. *'At turkey gobbled at everthang: crows, thunder, jaybirds. Hit was rail easy to course him.*

Cuss-out—The very worst kind of verbal abuse. *I didn't mind when Joker was jest a'cussin at me. But when he hauled off and cussed me out—and then cussed-out my Daddy too!—wale, thar warnt nuthin' to do but fight.*

Cyst—To provide assistance. *Nacherly, I was happy to hep when Doug ast me t'cyst him changin' a flat tar.*

D

D'rekly—Soon, in a short time. *I studied on 'at ciffern problem fer a while, and d'rekly the answer come to me.*

Dam—A rather mild cuss word. *Rhett Butler told Miss Scarlett he didn't give nary dam.* (See below for da-yum!)

Dark-thirty—Well after sunset. *Slim never would come home from a 'fishin' 'til dark-thirty.*

Dawg—Correct pronunciation of "dog," but usually reserved for hounds. *Kenny's beagle is one of the best rabbit dawgs in this here country.*

Da-yum!—Forceful expression of "damn." *Da-yum! Hit's snowed fer four days straight! We might not see sprang 'til the middle o'May!*

Deef—Hard of hearing. *Forney was so deef, he couldn't hear hit thunder.*

Did—The end of one's life. *Pore ol' Joe, he tuck a fever and now he's did.*

Dierear—Correct pronunciation of "diarrhea," also referred to as the "quick-steps." *Ever winter, a lot of dierear goes 'round in the schools.*

Dijikal—Of or relating to computer technology. *My seven-year-old grandson has fergot more about how to use 'at new dijikal stuff than I'll ever remember.*

Dilate—Live to a ripe old age before passing away. *At 103, Ain't Jenny shore didn't dilate.*

Dinner bucket—Lunchbox. *By any chance you gotta spair samich in yore dinner bucket?*

Disremember—Forget. *I disremember what I et fer dinner last Sunday.*

Dite—An attempt to lose weight. *Molly got so flashy Doc Lawson put her on a dite.*

Dob—A small amount. *Hit don't take but a little dob of Preparation H to cam yore asteroids.*

Don't care to—Correct pronunciation of "I don't mind at all," a very confusing term for many non-Southern Appalachians to grasp. *I don't care to drive you to work.*

Dope—Carbonated soft drink. *I'll take any kind of dope you got: grape, lemon, strawburry, Big Arnj, hit don't matter.*

Drank—Correct pronunciation of "drink." *Toby made up a drank with coffee, rum, grape jelly and prune juice. Da-yum! Hit warnt fit fer a dawg, much less a human bean!*

Drapped—Past tense of "drop." *Cletus drapped off to sleep inside of three mints.*

Drawed—Past tense of "drew." *Corneal drawed back on his compound bow and shot an arrol plum through a seven-point buck.*

Drearysome—Sad, lonely, desolate. *The woods shore look drearysome in November adder all 'em purty leaves have come down.*

Drownded—Correct pronunciation of "to drown." *One day when Fletcher was a'fishin' in North River, he stepped in a big hole and liked to drownded. They say he puked water fer two airs adderward.*

Drug—Past tense of "drag." *I know it warnt but a few hunnert yards, but I swear hit seems like I drug 'at deer four mile.*

Duddon—Correct pronunciation of "doesn't." *Duddon hit matter to you that Harvey quit school?*

E

Eats right whore you hold it—A high compliment for delicious food. *Ain't Polly's fried chicken eats right whore you hold it.*

Eggsample—Correct pronunciation of "example." *Gimme an eggsample of what yore a'tawlkin' about.*

Eggspeck—Anticipate. *We eggspeck Maude will git here afore dinner.*

Eggspurt—Authority on any topic. *Hershell was such an eggspurt at cifferin' he could figure out most thangs in his head.*

Elem—A large deciduous tree often found in cities. *I shore do like to park my truck under a shady elem on hot summer days.*

'em—Correct pronunciation of "them." *Ast 'em if they node whore Tammy went.*

Enemy—Medical procedure to alleviate temporary gastrointestinal blockage. *Adder I et all 'at cheese and got plugged up, ol' Doc Jones give me an enemy.*

Epizooticks—An unidentified and sometimes unmentioned disease. *When Hortense come down with the "sociable epizooticks," Doc Jenkins made a salve outta lard and camphor and rubbed it on her gentiles.*

Et—Past tense of "eat." *'At is the best creamed corn I nearly ever et.*

Ever—Correct pronunciation of "every." *Ever time I see iris flares in bloom, I think of Maw.*

Everbidy—Correct pronunciation of "everyone." *Everbidy in town node Sally was bad to take a little nip afore church.*

Everthang—Correct pronunciation of "everything." *Timmy throwed everthang but the kitchen sink and still didn't catch nary trout.*

Everwitch—Correct pronunciation of "which ever." *Everwitch way you want to go is fine by me.*

Eyeful Tar—Famous landmark in France. *Joe Billy seed the Eyeful Tar when he was in the Army.*

Eyegod!—An forceful exclamation, considered irreverent in some circles. *Eyegod, I called 'at no-good Yancey Brown a sumbich to his face, and eyegod he tuck it!*

F

Fallin' out—A disagreement. *Mary Ellen and Eugenia had a big fallin' out over Billy and never spoke airy word to un'nuther again.*

Fanger—Part of the human hand. *Jeff drove his tractor so slow on the highway, everbidy would give him the fanger.*

Far—Correct pronunciation of "fire." *Junior's barn caught far, but he was able to snuff hit out afore his hay burnt up.*

Fard—To be abruptly relieved of duty, often because of poor performance. *Lonzo called in sick one too many times, and they fard his lazy ass.*

Farn—Any distant location, usually across the ocean. *David said when he got in the Army and went to farn countries, nobody talked rite.*

Fartar—A building the government erects on ridgetops to detect woodland blazes. *Ever summer, Pete would drive to Montana and work in a fartar.*

Febairy—Second month of the year. *Febairy shore is a drearysome month.*

Fer—Correct pronunciation of "for." *Charlie'll win the 'rasslin' match fer shore.*

Fertilize—Correct pronunciation of "fertilizer." *Triple-ten fertilize is the best all-round to use on yore flares.*

Fetch—To give or produce. *Here, let me fetch some 'backer fer yore pipe.*

Fit—Past tense of "fight." *Wally and Hector fit and fit 'til they was plum give out.*

Fixin' to—Soon to commence. *You kin tell by the way his neck veins bulge that Jack is fixin' to lose his temper.*

Flare—Necessary ingredient in baking. *You can't make good biscuits without good flare.*

Flares—Correct pronunciation of "flowers." *Maw usta put flares on Paw's grave ever Easter.*

Flashy—Polite expression for obese; i.e., "fleshy." *Pearlie Mae has a sweet face, but she shore is flashy.*

For—Because. *Jonah allus made top dollar for he was the best ditch digger in these parts.*

Foot feed—Automobile accelerator. *Keep a'stompin' on 'at foot feed! Them James boys is a'ketchin' up with us! I node you shouldn't a'shot 'em the fanger back thar!*

Forty-leven—A rather large, but not inconceivable, number. *Dexter allus had forty-leven excuses fer not workin'.*

Fotched—Past tense of "fetch." *Sandy had his dawg so well-trained, it fotched everthang he shot, squirrels to quail.*

Frash—Correct pronunciation of "fresh." *Billy Joe was a'gittin' frash with Irene, so she hauled off and slapped the far outta him.*

Funnin'—To tease or joke. *It was allus hard to tell if Mr. Brickey was funnin' or tellin' the truth.*

Fur piece—A long distance. *When he done my colonoscopy, Doc Winters shore went a fur piece!*

G

Gap—The gate on a fence. *Be shore to close 'at gap adder you drive the tractor through.*

Garntee—Absolute. *Cas would allus garntee his watermelons were the best in town.*

Gentiles—Private parts of the human body. *Ferd was too embarrassed to show his gentiles to the nurse.*

Georgie—State due south of Tennessee. *My first cuzzin on Daddy's side—his name is Rupert but he goes by "Wildroot"—he lives in Hot Sprangs, Georgie.*

Git—Correct pronunciation of "get." *Tilda couldn't wait to git a job in Atlanta.*

Give—Relieve flatulence loudly. *Adder a big bate of pinto beans, Horace would give—and hit allus liked to peeled the wallpaper!*

Give out—Completely exhausted. *Adder he split four truckloads of farwood, Earl was plum give out.*

Go in with—Share the cost. *If you'd go in with me and Harry, we could buy 'at mule.*

Goan—Correct pronunciation of "going." *Rupert said he was goan to his Maw's house fer dinner.*

Gobullion—A large number, virtually beyond calculation. *They was a gobullion ducks a'swimmin' on 'at pond afore Ray snuck up and fard into 'em.*

Goober—1. Peanuts. *Cal allus liked to put goobers in his dopes.* 2. A lamebrain. *What a goober Harvey is!*

Goodurn—Correct pronunciation of "good one," meaning anything that excels. *Bob's oldest son has shore turned out to be a goodurn.*

Goozle, aka **swallerpipe**—Throat. *Willum almost smothered when he got a fish bone hung in his goozle.*

Grabblin'—The old mountain sport of catching catfish and snapping turtles with bare hands, often performed in the company of liquor. *Junior and Charlie only lost two fangers when they went a'grabblin' last Wednesday.*

Granny wommin—Midwife. *Better go fetch 'at granny wommin; Josephine is about to show.*

Graveyard did—A quick and certain death. *When Hank retched fer his pistol, Shurf Wayland shot him graveyard did.*

Groan—Correct pronunciation of "growing." *Maggie was groan a fine mess of pole beans 'til hit quit rainin.' Then the dadgum thangs jest dried up.*

Growed—Past tense of "grow." *Justin shore growed a fine 'mater crop this summer.*

Guessimate—A close estimate. *I'd guessimate Little Eva tips 'em scales at about 225 pound.*

Guvermit—Any local, state or federal entity. *They'll arrest yore ass fer steppin' one foot on guvermit property.*

H

Haint—1. Correct pronunciation of "is not." 2. A ghost. *Maude haint afeered of haints.*

Hair yew?—Correct pronunciation of "how are you?" *Hair yew, Mister Tom?*

Hale—Place bad people go after they die. *Ever August, hit's hotter'n the hinges of Hale around here.*

Hale far!—Expression of surprise or anger. *Hale far! I ain't seed you in a month of Sundays!*

Half-bad—So-so, acceptable and always preceded by "ain't." *Yore never gonna be no millionaire, but the pay down at the feed store ain't half-bad.*

Hard—Past tense of "hire." *Stevie got hard on night shift down at the Sebmblebm.*

Hare—What grows upon the head. *Mort looks like a wolf; he shore needs to git his hare cut.*

Hateful—A thing or a person that is obnoxious, irritating, ill-tempered, evil or mean. *'Em hateful skeeters are so bad this year, I done 'bout slapped my arms off.*

Hawg—Animal, domestic or wild, that produces pork. *Luke kilt a boar hawg that'ud weigh 350 pound.*

Heerd—Past tense of "hear." *I heerd you and Cathy was a'fixin' to have a youngin'—congratulations!*

Heidi—Proper greeting between friends and strangers alike. *Heidi, Miz Jones! You a'feelin' all right today?*

Hell—Contraction for "he will." *Hell work out jest fine in the Navy.*

Hep—To assist. *When his house caught far, all of Bud's neighbors turned out to hep any way possible.*

He-pin—A vast amount. *Burl's breath smelled like a goat adder he et a he-pin bate of ramps.*

Hern—Correct pronunciation of "hers." *Sally swore 'at samich was hern, so I give it back.*

Herring—A basic human perceptive sense involving the ears. *Might as well cut off Jode's years; his herring's gone.*

Hesh—Be quiet. *Willadeen yammers so much—if she would jest hesh you could still hear her echo fer two airs!*

Het up—1. Prepare leftover food for eating. *Let's het up 'at chicken fer supper.* 2. Anger. *Laurie gits het up over the slightest thang.*

Hire—Continually greater elevation. *Buster clem hire and hire 'til he retched the crest of the ridge.*

Hisn—Correct pronunciation of "his." *Jody said 'at tackle box was hisn.*

Hisself—Correct pronunciation of "himself." *Jessie shore was proud of hisself fer winnin' 'at foot race.*

Hissy—A tantrum, spat, argument. *Ellen was bad to throw a hissy if her boyfriend was late.*

Hit—Correct pronunciation of "it." *Hit shore looks like rain today.*

Hole—A vast or entire amount. *When Earl scored a touchdown late in the game, the hole crowd jumped and hollered rail loud.*

Holler—A steep mountain valley. *Bart lives so far up 'at holler, hit don't hardly git daylight 'til noon.*

Horticulture—Social lessons offered to a woman of ill repute. *You kin lead a horticulture, but you can't learn her how to hold a teacup.*

Human bean—Person. *I wouldn't go out with Julie if she was the last human bean on this planet!*

Hunkers—A squatted position. *David was a'sittin' on his hunkers in front of the far, tryin' to warm up.*

Hunnert—The number immediately following ninety-nine. *Hit must be a hunnert degrees today!*

I

Ideal—An inspiration, often sudden. *Ben Franklin had the bright ideal to fly a kite in the middle of a thunderstorm.*

Idjit—A fool, moron. *Quit actin' like an idjit and git in here outta the rain!*

Idnit—Correct pronunciation of "isn't it?" *Idnit a purty sunrise!*

Ignert—Lacking any sense, common or otherwise. *Boy, 'at Jones feller is so ignert, I don't see how he ties his own shoes!*

I-swan—To lightly swear in polite company. *I-swan if a bire didn't jest run acrost the trail up ahead!*

Ill—Bad-tempered, quick to anger. *He was ill as a stepped-on snake.*

Ima-goan—Common phrase related to "fixin' to." *Ima-goan whup yore ass if you don't hesh!*

Ittle—Correct pronunciation of "it will." *Ittle quit rainin' one of these days.*

J

Jake-lag—Crippling condition from longtime consumption of moonshine. *Freddie got jake-lag so bad, they had to send him to the vetrin's home in Johnson City.*

Jaw—Idle conversation. *Robb would jaw all night 'less everbidy started standin' up and a'yawnin' rail big.*

Jaybird—Swim without clothes. *I'll go jaybird if you will.*

Jeet—Much shorter phrase to speak than, "Have you already taken a meal?" *Jeet yet?*

Jew—Proper negative reply for the previous question. *No, jew?*

Jew-here?—An inquiry. *Jew-here Claude was a'movin' outta town?*

Jest—Correct pronunciation of "just." *Now you wait jest a minute thar, mister!*

Jine—Correct pronunciation of "join." *I shore wish he'd jine us fer dinner.*

Job—Correct pronunciation of "jab." *When yawnin' didn't work, somebody'd have to job a fanger in Robb's belly and tell him to jest hesh!*

K

Kant-helpits—Sickness. *Helen tuck to sneezin' and a'coughin' and the next thang you node, she come down with a bad case of the kant-helpits.*

Keep yeself—Abstain from sex. *The preacher told Allen, "The Lord eggspecks you to keep yeself 'til you and Lois git hitched."*

Ketched—Past tense of "catch." *Ken ketched all 'em bass on topwater plugs.*

Kilt—Past tense of "kill." *They's a law that says you need to call the shurf when somebody gits kilt, even if they deserved killin'.*

Kin—Correct pronunciation of "can." *We kin all go to Newport next weekend.*

Kindly—Approximately, sort of. *I'm kindly worried about Helen.*

Kivvers—Bedspread. *Pull up 'em kivvers! I'm 'bout half froze to death!*

L

Lag—Body part used for walking and running. *I shore hope her lag ain't broke.*

Lane—In a reclining position. *Butch's head hurts, so he's lane on the bed fer a few minutes.*

'Lasses aka **sa'grum**—Molasses, always spoken in plural. *These are some of the best 'lasses 'at ever went down my swallerpipe.*

Law—Put someone under arrest. *They lawed Amos fer makin' likker.*

Learnt—To gain knowledge. *Miss Vesser, she learnt me English rail good.*

Least—Smallest. *Nancy is the least girl in first grade. Pore thang. Why I bet she don't weigh 30 pound!*

Lectrick—Correct pronunciation of "electricity." *TVA brung us the lectrick in 1943.*

Let out—Come to a close, adjourn. *When Preacher Mosely gits wound up on far and brimstone, church don't hardly let out 'til 2 o'clock.*

LIB—Common term of surprise; i.e.,"Well, I'll be!" *LIB! Sally and Earl bought 'at house over on Elem Street!*

Lieberry—A vast repository of books available to the public on loan. *The lieberry is one of my favorite places to roam and look fer colyum ideas.*

Light a shuck—Make haste. *You better light a shuck if you want to finish afore dark.*

Light bread—Store-bought bread. *Light bread makes better samiches than cornbread.*

Likker—Correct pronunciation of "liquor." *The Baptists never speak to each other in likker stores.*

Long Tom–Single-shot shotgun with a barrel 36 inches or more in length. *Warnt nary squirrel could climb so high 'at Carl's Long Tom couldn't retch him.*

Longhandles–Insulated underwear. *I allus need longhandles 'round the middle of October.*

M

Mammaries—Remembrances. *Some of my fondest school mammaries are from Miz Johnson's class in the sixth grade.*

Marred—To become immersed in. *Scott drove offen the road and got marred up to his axles.*

Mater—Delicious garden vegetable that ripens in mid-summer. *Nothin I like better'n a mater samich on light bread.*

Mayzur—Correct pronunciation of "measure." *You mayzur thangs with a ruler or yardstick.*

Mere—Reflective surface found in bathrooms. *I can't shave 'less I'm a'lookin' in the mere.*

Mess—A sufficient supply. *Irene picked a mess of collards.*

Mikerscope—An instrument for seeing small objects. *Doc Cannon bought a mikerscope fer his office. Now he kin run his own testis and don't have to send 'em to 'at lab in Nashville.*

Minners—Small fish. *Creek minners are shore good bate fer crappies and bass.*

Mint—Time period of 60 seconds. *I'll feed the dawg in jest a mint.*

Morn—Correct pronunciation of "more than." *His ol' car won't hold morn a couple of quarts of all.*

Mouth—1. Sassy backtalk. *Much more of 'at mouth and yore a'gittin' a whuppin,' young feller!* 2. The distinctive cry of a hound. *Ol' Blue had better mouth than airy redbone in this county.*

Move-bull—Flexible and often interchangeable materials. *Why, I bet Herb's '48 Ford coupe had 10,000 move-bull parts!*

N

Nacherly—Correct pronunciation of "naturally." *Nacherly, Paul retched fer the biggest pork chop on the platter.*

Nanner—Yellow fruit that grows in bunches. *Elvis loved fried nanner samiches.*

Narrol—A tight, closely confined space. *They's a narrol, windin' road up to Uncle Lynn's place.*

Nary—Correct pronunciation of "not any." *They was nary doughnut to be found adder Sunday School let out.*

Nekkid—Unclothed (and generally up to hanky-panky.) *Uncle Fred saw Sonny and Barbara Jean nekkid down at the swimmin' hole.*

New ground—Freshly cleared land. *Rollie's new ground must mayzur 10 acres!*

'nm—Common term meaning "everyone else, all others." *Ast Bill 'nm if they'd like to eat dinner with us.*

Node—Past tense of "know." *He node the answer all along.*

Nunnia—Correct pronunciation of "none of your." *Hit's nunnia dam bidness what I thank!*

Nuthin'ud do—Never satisfied. *I done tuck Sarie to one pitcher show, but nuthin'ud do her but go to ever dadblame one 'at comes to town.*

O

Of a mind–Determined. *I've of a mind to kick my boss in his butt.*

Off-bare–Laborer at a sawmill who removes and stacks boards as they come off the carriage; i.e, "off-bearer." *Punkin got hisself hard as an off-bare at Big Ed's sawmill.*

Offen–1. Correct pronunciation of "often." *How offen you git to town?* 2. Remove. *Git offen me!*

Okry–Garden vegetables that grow in green pods. *I could eat my weight in fried okry.*

Ol'–Generally a term of affection added to any person, place or object. *Ol' Henry, he's gotta heart of pure gold.*

Old timers disease–A cruel neurological ailment, mostly among the elderly. *Uncle Harmon had old timers disease and got to whore he couldn't even remember his own name.*

Onct–Correct pronunciation of "once." *Fairy tales always begin with "onct upon a time."*

Orifice–A place where city people work. *Silas's daddy worked in a big orifice downtown.*

Ovair–Correct pronunciation of "over there." *Ronnie said he was jest a'goan ovair fer a few mints.*

P

Painter—Mountain lion. *Carson swore he seed a painter but nobody ever believed him.*

Panch—A small amount. *You jest need a panch of salt in 'at bobacue sauce.*

Pare—Electricity delivered through wires. *Hit's supposed to be rail cold this winter; I bet my pare bill's gonna be outta sight!*

Parson—Correct pronunciation of "person." *Anytime Preacher Cook ast fer more money, ever parson in church dug a little deeper.*

Past—Correct pronunciation of "passed." *Moody stomped the foot feed and past Boomer's truck like hit was a'standin' still!*

Pastor—A field for livestock. *They's aplenty of hay fer the cows in the back pastor.*

Peckerwood—1. Birds that cling to tree trunks and feed behind the bark. *They was a red-headed peckerwood in my hickories last week.* 2. A slightly derogatory term. *George is such a peckerwood!*

Pillar—Bed item where the head is rested. *I can't sleep without my own pillar.*

Piney flares—Correct pronunciation of "peony." *Miss Mary Ann grows the purtiest piney flares you ever seed.*

Pitcher—Correct pronunciation of "picture." *I seed yore pitcher in the paper last Monday.*

Pizen—Correct pronunciation of "poison." *I wouldn't eat 'at meat—hit's been settin' out all day and is liable to be pizen.*

Plars—A common grasping/holding tool found in many workshops. *'Em dam plars slipped, and I liked to panched a hole in my fangers.*

Playzur—Engage in sexual relations, often outside of wedlock. *Melody and Mike are bad to playzur with un'nuther when Marvin and Millie are out of town.*

Please—Law-enforcement officers found in municipal areas. *David is the chief of please in our town.*

Plum—Completely. *I'm plum wore out from a'walkin' to town.*

Pore—Lacking financial means. *They was pore as Job's turkey.*

Pound—A measure of weight, always expressed singularly regardless of amount. *I bet 'at big rock'll go a good 250 pound.*

Punkin—A large, orange fruit associated with Halloween. *Adder they wrote nice stuff about Hiram in the newspaper, his head swole up bigger'n a $15 punkin.*

Pure-T—An adjective added for special emphasis, good or bad. *Onct Lillian's daughter growed up, she was pure-T gorgeous! 'At was the pure-T worst coffee ever I drunk!*

Purty—1. Attractive. *Mary Louise shore has a purty baby.* 2. Approximate. *I purty-near got a limit of bass.*

Q

Quare—1. Odd, unusual, different (with no sexual connotations whatsoever.) *Rusty shore is turned quare.* 2. A musical group often associated with churches. *My wife sangs in the quare.*

Quiled—Coiled. *I seed a four-foot rattlesnake quiled up on Junior's front porch!*

R

Raddeo—Correct pronunciation of "radio." *I allus keep my raddeo tuned to WDVX, 89.9.*

Raglar—Correct pronunciation of "regular." *My bass boat runs best on plain ol' raglar gas, not that high-test stuff.*

Rail—Exceedingly. *Floyd caught a rail big catfish.*

Ranch—1. A tool. *I need a ¾-inch ranch.* 2. Bodily harm occurring during an accident. *He fell on ice last Tuesday and liked to ranch his knee somethin' awful.* 3. Hair color, especially for women. *Down at the beauty parlor, Miz Williams ast fer blue ranch 'stead of the usual red.*

Rang—Correct pronunciation of "wring." *Go out and rang a chicken's neck, and we'll shore eat good tonight!*

Rasslin'—Correct pronunciation of "wrestling." *Some people say TV rasslin' is fake.*

Rat—Right, often followed by "cheer." *Rat cheer is whore Rufe got kilt, all rat.*

Ready-roll—A commercially produced cigarette, often considered lavish among grow-it-yourself mountaineers. *Nuthin' I hate more'n hearin' a man complain about bein' broke when he's a'standin' thar a'smokin' a ready-roll.*

Real eyes—To become suddenly aware of. *Now I real eyes what she was a'cryin' about! Her husband had done walked out!*

Retard—To voluntarily leave a job, especially after long service. *Bubba retard adder 35 years at the Oakdale Far Hall.*

Retch—Correct pronunciation of "reach." *Please retch over yonder and fetch me 'at hammer.*

Right smart of—Large amount. *"He owns a right smart of land in Sevier County.*

Rite—Creating or conveying a story on paper. *Adder he's had a few dranks of likker, ol' Venable shore kin rite colyums good!*

Rozinears—Correct pronunciation of "roasting ears," i.e., sweet corn. *Lucy biled six rozinears, and they et right whore you held 'em.*

Runt—Destroyed. *Yeah, but she biled 'em 'taters 'til they's plum runt!*

S

Sailor—Modern device for personal communication. *Billy carries a sailor phone in the front pocket of his overalls.*

Sale—Tiny units of life in plants and animals. *In bygolligy class, Mr. Reed showed us how to cut a tater rail thin so we could see its sales under a mikerscope.*

Samich—Two pieces of light bread with meat. *Mary Nell makes the best ham samich you nearly ever et.*

Sar—Correct pronunciation of "sour." *Whew! 'Em green apples shore are sar!*

Saucerd'nblowed—The old country method of cooling coffee. (A small amount was poured from the cup into a saucer, slowly and carefully blown across, then consumed directly from the saucer.) *Pa Dougherty allus saucerd'nblowed his coffee afore hit was fit t'drank.*

Sebmblebm—Chain of convenience stores often found in cities. *I gotta run down to the Sebmblebm and buy me a pack of Marlboros.*

Secretion—A story or fact hidden from others. *Florence had a deep, dark secretion.*

Seed—Past tense of "see." *I seed you a'pickin' blackburries 'tuther day.*

Settin—In a seated position. *Marvin is a'settin over yonder in a rockin' cheer.*

Sex—Correction pronunciation of the number 6. *Jake owed him sex dollars.*

Shangles—Shingles, either rain-proofing materials for a roof or a painful medical condition. *Lonnie was a'makin' shangles in his backyard, but dam if his shangles didn't flare up and he tuck to his bed.*

Share—Stand-up bath. *In the summer, you art to take a share at least onct a day.*

Shed—Discard. *Wilbur's beagle is too lazy to run rabbits; he art to git shed of hit.*

Sheyit—A mild-to-strong cuss word. *Well, sheyit! Darlene done drapped a good dinner plate and broke hit plum into forty-leven pieces!*

Shore—An affirmative answer. *I shore would be proud to take Miss Ruthie to the dance.*

Shuck—Correct pronunciation of "shook." *Benny shuck 'at tree 'til a squirrel dropped out.*

Shurf—Highest elective law-enforcement officer in any given county. *Andy says he's gonna run fer shurf. Might as well. He's done run from him enough!*

Sine—A large message board, often associated with highway travel. *Didn't we jest pass the sine fer Route 36?*

Sinner—In the middle. *His arrol hit smack dab in the sinner of the bull's-eye.*

Sisk—A painful inflammation on the skin. *Doc Smith had to lance the sisk on Ricky's arm.*

Skeerce—Correct pronunciation of "scarce." *Money has got so skeerce these days, I may have to go on welfare.*

Skeeter—Correct pronunciation of "mosquito." *I got a skeeter bite on my lag the size of a quarter.*

Skraddle—A private area of the human body; i.e., crotch. *Newt keeps scratchin' at his skraddle; his gentiles must itch somethin' awful.*

Smack dab—With great precision. *He fell 12 foot outta 'at elem tree but landed smack dab on his feet!*

Smother—Suffocate. *Open up 'at winder; I'm about to smother.*

Soot—Fancy men's clothing. *Cletus went to Walmart and bought hisself a new soot.*

Spashul—Correct pronunciation of "special." *I hope I git somethin' spashul on my birthday.*

Spair—Extra. *Larry went to change his flat tar, but dam if the spair warnt flat too!*

Spale—1. An unspecific period of time. *I ain't seed her in quite a spale.* 2. Correct arrangement of letters in a word. *Marleene was so dumb, she couldn't spale "cat" if you spotted her the "c" and the "t."*

Spearmint—A scientific test. *Herman worked over at Oak Ridge so long, they had to do spearmints on his pee ever six to eight month.*

Sprang—Season of the year between winter and summer. *All our flares start comin' up in the sprang.*

Sprankle—Small drops of water. *The Presbyteruns, 'Pisscopalians and Methodiss sprankle; the Babliss dunk full bore.*

Squarsh—1. To mash. *I'm gonna squarsh you like a roachbug!* 2. A garden vegetable. *Maw allus grows squarsh but I shore don't like to eat it.*

Squire—Correct pronunciation of "square." *The squire root of sixteen is four.*

Stank—Smell badly. *Buster shore does stank. I bet he ain't tuck a share all week!*

Stobbed—Correct pronunciation of "stabbed." *Floyd stobbed his knife plum through Grady's lag.*

Strang—A continuous length of threads or fine wire. *Fred busted a banjer strang while playin' "The Arnj Blossom Spashul."*

Stummick—Correct pronunciation of "stomach." *Adder vittles go down yore swallerpipe, they wind up in yore stummick.*

Sumbich—A coarse term to describe an unpleasant person. *Ralph's the biggest sumbich in this part of the state!*

Summers—Correct pronunciation of "somewhere." *I set 'em plars down here summers.*

Surp—Delicious sweet liquid from maple trees or sugar cane. *I love maple surp on my pancakes.*

T

Taint—Correct pronunciation of "is not." *Taint proper to kiss on the first date.*

Take up—Begin. *What time does school take up?*

Tal—Item used for personal drying. *They's nothing like a nice warm tal adder you step outta the share on a cold morning.*

Tar—Round objects on motor vehicles. *Yore truck will need four tars, 'less hit's one of 'em duallies; then hit'll need six.*

Tar tool—An implement used for tire repairs and sometimes as a weapon. *Allus keep a tar tool handy.*

Tard—Exhausted. *I'm so tard I believe I could go to sleep a'standin' up.*

Taters—Correct pronunciation of "potatoes." *Let's fry up a big skillet of taters.*

Tawlk—Correct pronunciation of "talk." *You kin tawlk to him 'til yore blue in the face, but hit won't do nary bit of good.*

Testis—Exams taken in school to get a grade. *We're gonna have 'em history testis next week, and I shore hope I've studied enough.*

Thang—Correct pronunciation of "thing." *To hear 'em Yankees tawlk, they don't know a dam thang!*

Thank—What you do with your brain. *I thank I'll run over to Fred's house fer a beer.*

Thar—Correct pronunciation of "there." *Jest set 'at box over thar.*

That'ud—Contracted form of "that would." *That'ud made a good board if it didn't have all 'em knots.*

Theirn—Correct pronunciation of "theirs." *The Whites said 'at cow warnt theirn.*

They—1. Common expression of mock surprise, often followed by "law." *They law, the freckles on 'at boy's face!* 2. Authoritative and unquestionable source on any and all matters. *They say Judge Winston ain't ever drawed a sober breath in his life.*

They's—Contracted form of "there is." *They's a'fixin to be a fight adder the card game.*

Thieve—To steal. *Don't leave yore billfold a'settin thar; hit'll git thieved shore as the world.*

Throwed—Past tense of "threw." *Jane guzzled her 'shine too fast and throwed up all over the cab of Mike's new pickup.*

Tolerble—Correct pronunciation of "tolerable," specifically in good running order. *Anytime you ast Doc Allen how he was a'doin' he allus said, "Oh, I'm tolerable."*

Tords—Correct pronunciation of "toward." *We gotta drive tords Bulls Gap to reach Granny's house.*

Tuba for—A common board used in construction. *Smitty needed jest one more tuba for to finish his outhouse.*

Tuck—Correct pronunciation of "took." *Ol' Slick, he tuck off a'runnin' like he done seed the devil hisself!*

Tush hawg—A bully. *One of these days, somebody's goan take 'at tush hawg down a few pegs.*

'tuther—Recently passed moment in time. *We went to a hawg-killin' 'tuther day.*

Twict—Two times. *I done told you chillens twict to hesh up and go to bed!*

U

Un'nuther—Many people. *The board members all got with un'nuther and decided to accept plans fer a new schoolhouse.*

Under-marry/over-marry—To wed far below or above one's social-economic-educational status. *My sister seriously under-married when she got hitched to Tony.*

Unquile—Correct pronunciation of "uncoil." *They must be forty-leven knots in this fishin' line; I don't know if hit'll ever unquile.*

Untellin'—Unfathomable. *Hit's untellin' how many shangles hit took to roof Uncle Arthur's barn.*

Up'n died—Passed away rather suddenly. *Larry worked a full day Monday and Tuesday, like nuthin' ever happened; then he jest up'n died Wednesday mornin'. Beats all I ever seed!*

Urine—One of five types of material possession. *They's mine, urine, hisn, hern, theirn: "'At money ain't urine, so give hit back!"*

V

Vars—1. Part of a song. *We'll sing the first vars of "The Old Rugged Cross."* 2. Sudden illness that often overtakes young children. *Shew! They's a vars a'runnin' through the third grade, and kids have throwed up all over the place!* 3. A wide variety. *Vars and sundry people live in New York City.*

Vetrin—A former member of the armed forces. *Barney had more war medals than airy vetrin ever I node.*

Vidock—A bridge that crosses a road or train tracks. *A four-car crash has closed the Oak Street vidock.*

Vittles—Food. *The vittles we et in the Air Force warnt half-bad.*

Vummick—Correct pronunciation of "vomit." *Junior et some bad aigs and vummicked all day.*

Vury—Correct pronunciation of "very." *Abidy has to look vury close to tell 'em Blankenship twins apart.*

W

Wale—A source of water in the country. *Wally had to dig over nine-hunnert feet to brang in his wale.*

Wangs—Bird parts. *Verlie et an entire platter of chicken wangs.*

War—What electrical power is delivered in. *Randolph ran a war from his bedroom to the TV.*

Warhouse—A large building for supplies. *When Sully moved off to Georgie, he worked at a tar warhouse.*

Warnt—Contraction of "were not." *We warnt goan on no vacation this summer.*

Warsh—Correct pronunciation of "wash." *Swing in 'at car warsh and let's hose the cow manure offen yore truck.*

Warshrag—Piece of cloth used for bathing. *They shore have fancy warshrags at the Holiday Inn.*

Wasper—Stinging insects. *Chris used a hole can of spray on 'at wasper nest.*

Wheelbar—Long-handled garden implement that rolls. *Molly filled her wheelbar with maters and okry.*

Whole—A large depression or circle. *Ollie's goose gun went off accidental and blowed a big whole in the barn. His ol' lady never let him fergit, neither.*

Whomperjawed—Seriously out of alignment. *Who taught Butch how to lay brick? Look, they're all whomperjawed!*

Whore—Correct pronunciation of "where." *Whore did you'ins go to school when you'ins was groan up?*

Whup—Correct pronunciation of "whip," as in beat. *The principal will whup him good fer a'whupping 'at Thompson boy adder gym class.*

Widder—Correct pronunciation of "widow." *I heerd Widder Jones has tuck a shine to Preacher Collins.*

Winder—Glass-paned opening in a building. *Leroy throwed a baseball and busted out a winder in the schoolhouse.*

Wommin—Females, singular or plural. *They shore is some purty wommin at the swimmin' hole.*

X

Xhell—Forcibly push breath out of the lungs. *Doc James poked a fanger into my gentiles, had me to cough rail loud, then told me it was OK to xhell. I shore wish I node what that had to do with coming in fer a flu shot!*

Xtree—Correct pronunciation of "extra." *Ever four years, Febairy gits an xtree day.*

Y

Yale—To shout loudly. *When I was a boy, the only way to tawlk long-distance was to stand on one ridge and yale over to the next 'un.*

Yaller—A pleasant color. *Martha's hare was yaller as corn silks.*

Year—One of two appendages on the head used for hearing. *I node 'em artist fellers was all crazy, but one guy named Van Go cut offen his own year!*

Yestiddy—One day previous. *Hank left yestiddy to visit his sister in Georgie.*

Yonna—Correct pronunciation for "Do you wish to?" *Yonna swim jaybird?*

Yore—Preferred spelling of "your" and "you're." *Does yore pappy say hit's OK to go to town?*

You'ins—Collection term for "everybody," similar to "youse" spoken by Yankees. *You'ins come on in this here house and set a spell.*

Yurp—A large continent. *Uncle Elmore and Ain't Nellie went to Yurp fer their 50th anniversary.*

Z

Zacklies—Similar, approximate, precise. *I disremember the zacklies of how to git to Imogene's house.*

Zat—Correct pronunciation of "Is that?" *Zat the cow Uncle Robert was a'lookin' fer?*

Zillun—Slightly smaller amount than a gobullion. *If I already had a zillun dollars, I wouldn't be 'ritin' these silly books!*

ABOUT THE AUTHOR

Sam Venable is a humorist, newspaper columnist, outdoor writer, standup comedian and author of 12 books. He has worked for the Knoxville (Tenn.) News Sentinel since 1970, after having served as a staff member of the Knoxville Journal and Chattanooga News-Free Press. He is a member of the East Tennessee Writers Hall of Fame and Tennessee Journalism Hall of Fame. His website is samvenable.com.

Both he and his wife, Mary Ann, are graduates of the University of Tennessee. She is a retired UT software instructor. They frequently lead Smoky Mountain Field School courses on Southern Appalachian humor, dialect and heritage. Sam and Mary Ann live in a log house atop a wooded ridge on the outskirts of Knoxville. They are the parents of two adult children and two young grandchildren.

Made in the USA
Charleston, SC
26 August 2016